Contents

CW00461109

* C = copper; B = bronze; T = teacher; ( ) = the line must be played but cannot be assessed for a Medal.

Line Dance

Colin Cowles

AB 3221

Keeping Things Simple

Christopher Norton

AB 3221

When the Saints go Marching in

James M. Black & Katherine Purvis
arr. Alan Haughton

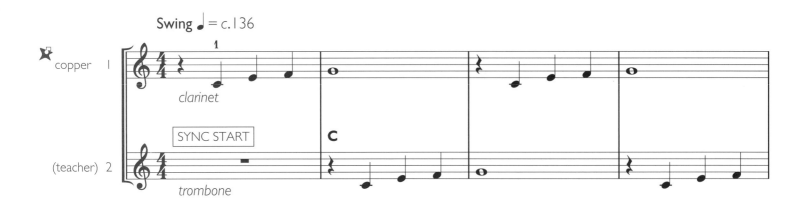

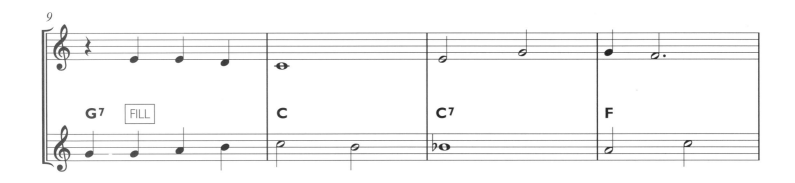

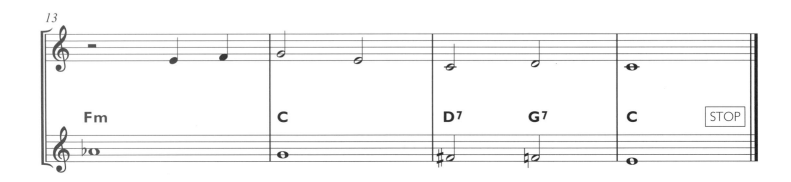

AB 3221

Lollipops

Louise Cook

Just a Breeze

Mike Cornick

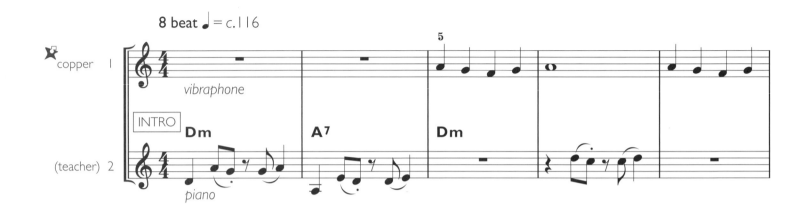

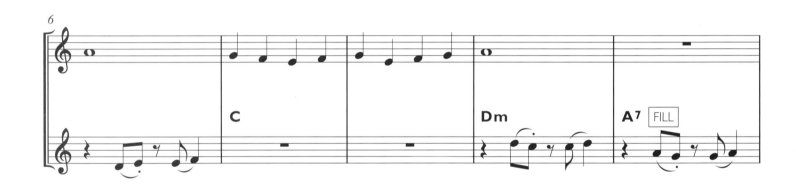

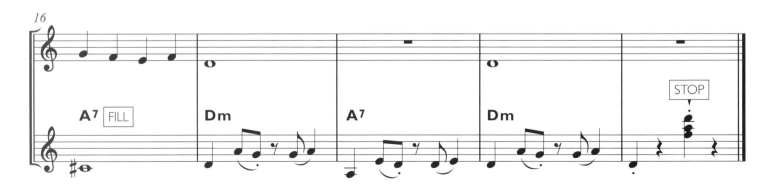

AB 3221

Shock-Horror Rock

Jane Sebba

* Sing or speak the words before you learn the piece, then think the words as you play.

Angel Fish

Sarah Walker

AB 3221

Done and Dusted

John Caudwell

Mattachins

from *Orchésographie* (1588)

Arbeau
arr. Jane Sebba

AB 3221

Summer Swing

Louise Cook

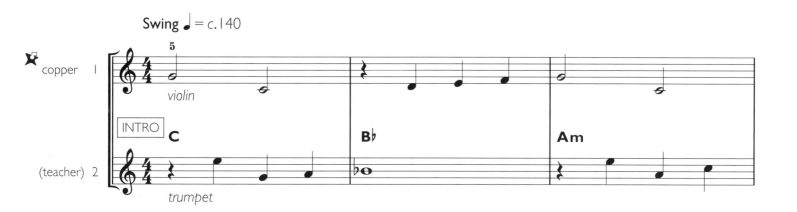

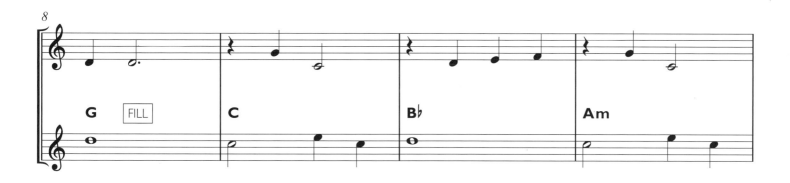

Bopping on the Bus

Nigel Penfold

AB 3221

Sweet Dreams

Alan Haughton

AB 3221

Toad in the Hole

Andrew Eales

Dance till Morning

Nancy Litten

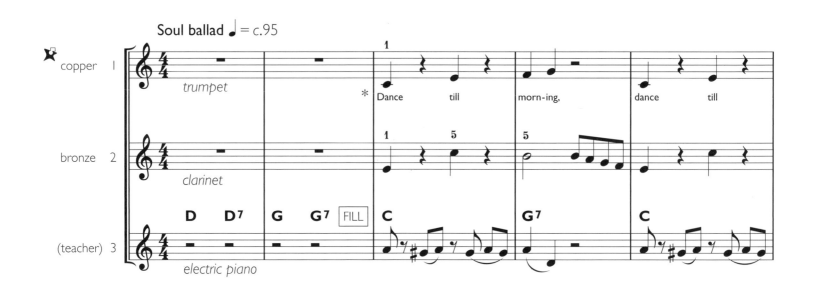

* Sing or speak the words before you learn the piece, then think the words as you play.

AB 3221

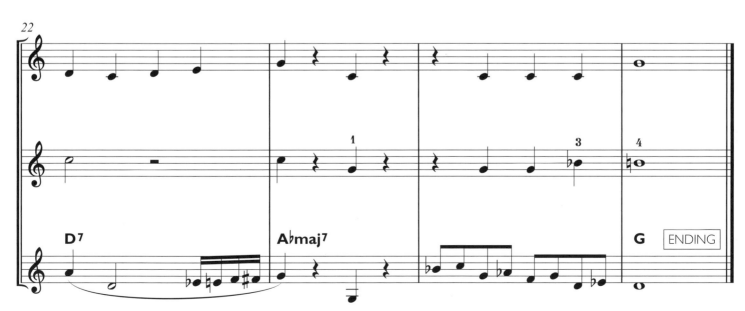

Pass the Ball

Jane Sebba

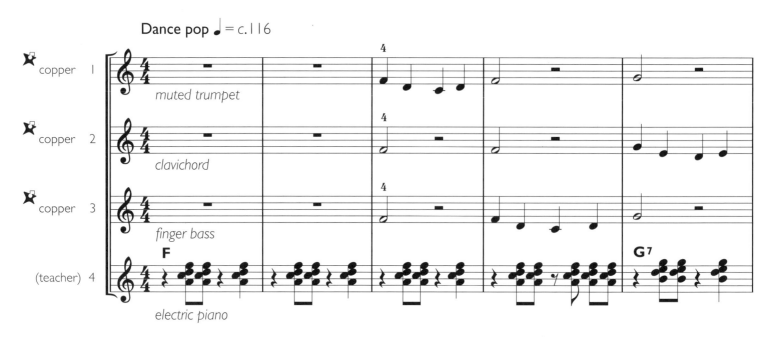

AB 3221